The Prodigal Father

The Prodigal Father

Angelo Scarano

LITURGICAL PRESS
Collegeville, Minnesota

www.litpress.org

Originally published in 2012 as *O marnotratném Otci* © Karmelitánské nakladatelství s.r.o., Kostelní Vydří 2012, Czech Republic, www.kna.cz. Translation by Pavlina and Tim Morgan.

1   2   3   4   5   6   7   8   9

Library of Congress Cataloging-in-Publication Data

Scarano, Angelo.
  [O marnotratném Otci. English]
  The prodigal father / Angelo Scarano.
    pages cm
  Includes bibliographical references.
  ISBN 978-0-8146-4924-4 (pbk.) — ISBN 978-0-8146-4949-7 (ebook)
    1. Prodigal son (Parable)   I. Title.

  BT378.P8S2313   2015
  226.8'06—dc23   2014023487

Contents

Introduction

*D*ante described Luke as the evangelist of Christ's gentleness and compassion.[1] Luke's gospel does indeed contain a number of passages about compassion, and one of these, the "pearl of all parables," the "gospel within the gospel,"[2] is the parable of the Prodigal Son (Luke 15:11-32). But is it really *the parable of the Prodigal Son*? Many biblical scholars take issue with this title and suggest alternatives, such as the Lost Son, the Two Sons, or more often the Merciful Father or the Waiting Father.

At first the story appears quite straightforward and easy to understand. Its true meaning can be obscured, however, by at least four commonly held fallacies, which suggest that

1. it is a parable about a *prodigal son*, so the main character is the younger son;

2. the younger son is a prime example of a repentant sinner who "comes to his senses," regrets his past, and confesses his sin;

3. the father in the story represents "God the Father";

4. the parable's message is aimed primarily at the "tax collectors and sinners."

However, although each of these assumptions contains a grain of truth, we will gradually refute each one of them.

There is an amusing passage in Graham Greene's *Monsignor Quixote*,[3] in which Father Quixote is discussing Luke's gospel with the Communist mayor, Sancho, who manages to turn the familiar story completely inside out:

> "A very beautiful parable," Father Quixote said with a note of defiance. He felt uneasy about what was to come.
>
> "Yes, it begins very beautifully," said the Mayor. "There is this very bourgeois household, a father and two sons. One might describe the father as a rich Russian kulak who regards his peasants as so many souls whom he owns."
>
> "There is nothing about kulaks or souls in the parable."
>
> "The story you have read has been probably a little corrected and slanted here and there by ecclesiastical censors."
>
> "What do you mean?"
>
> "It could have been told so differently and perhaps it was. Here is this young man who by some beneficent trick of heredity has grown up against all odds with a hatred of inherited wealth. . . . The son feels stifled by his bourgeois surroundings—perhaps even by the kind of furniture and the kind of pictures on the walls, of fat kulaks sitting down to their Sabbath meal, a sad contrast with the poverty he sees around him. He has to escape—anywhere. So he demands his share of the inheritance which will come to his brother and himself on their father's death and leaves home."
>
> "And squanders his inheritance in wild living," Father Quixote interrupted.
>
> "Ah, that's the official version. My version is that he was so disgusted by the bourgeois world in which he had been

brought up that he got rid of his wealth in the quickest way possible—perhaps he even gave it away and in a Tolstoyian gesture he became a peasant."

"But he came home."

"Yes, his courage failed him. He felt very alone on the pig farm. There was no branch of the Party to which he could look for help. *Das Kapital* had not yet been written, so he was unable to situate himself in the class struggle. Is it any wonder that he wavered for a time, poor boy? . . . Oh, he is welcomed home that's true enough, a fatted calf is served, he is probably happy for a few days, but then he feels again the same oppressive atmosphere of bourgeois materialism that drove him from home. His father tries to express his love, but the furniture is still hideous, false Louis Quinze or whatever was the equivalent in those days, the same pictures of good living are on the walls, he is shocked more than ever by the servility of the servants and the luxury of the food, and he begins to remember the companionship he found in the poverty of the pig farm. . . .

"After a week of disillusion he leaves home at dawn (a red dawn) to find again the pig farm and the old bearded peasant, determined now to play his part in the proletarian struggle. The old bearded peasant sees him coming from a distance and, running up, he throws his arms around his neck and kisses him, and the Prodigal Son says, "Father, I have sinned, I am not worthy to be called your son.""

This amusing attempt at "interpretation" shows that when a text is approached with closed ears and the mind already made up, God's word can quickly and easily be twisted to suit our own ideas. But we should not change God's word to suit us—the word should, instead, transform us.

1

The Context of the Story

When interpreting any parable, knowing the context is paramount, and this includes knowledge of both the setting and the intended audience. The question the Pharisees had asked at the banquet at Matthew the tax collector's house—"Why do you eat and drink with tax collectors and sinners?" (Luke 5:30)—returns here with fresh significance. The Pharisees once more reproach Jesus for welcoming sinners and eating with them (see Luke 15:2), and Jesus responds by telling them three parables of "the lost"—the Lost Sheep, the Lost Coin, and the Prodigal Son (see Luke 15). The common theme in all three parables in Luke chapter 15 is rejoicing at finding something or someone that had been "lost," and this rejoicing is then experienced to the full at a banquet for the "sinners."

But for whom is this parable primarily intended? Is Jesus perhaps telling it to sinners? The answer can be found in the text itself: "So he told *them* this parable," and in this case "them" refers to the "grumbling" Pharisees (15:2, 3). So in actual fact it is not so much an appeal to sinners as to the hard-hearted righteous. The "sinners" have already been rejoicing at being together with Jesus; they have already experienced the return home. They did not need to hear a figurative story because they were already experiencing the reality of being readmitted as "sons." Instead, it was the hard-hearted and self-righteous, full of anger and bitterness and refusing to go in to celebrate, who needed to hear the call to return to the father's house.[1]

The final section of the parable also shows that the intended hearers are the "righteous" who believe that they—like the elder son—have never broken a single rule. It is the closing words of biblical passages that often betray the writer's intention, and this parable does not conclude with the younger son's welcome home, but with the father's conversation with the elder son. Furthermore, the conversation is left open-ended: it is up to the hearers, the Pharisees, who grumble like the elder son, to make their own response to Jesus' invitation. The banquet is for them also, but only on condition that they accept the "sinners" as their brothers.

Jesus responds to this grumbling by explaining, through the parable, his attitude toward the common sinner, symbolized by the younger son. The father in the parable does not, therefore, first and foremost symbolize God the Father, but Jesus Christ himself. Because the parable explains and defends Christ's attitude toward sinners, it is Christ who is the "merciful father."[2] Christ, through his concern for and kindness toward those who go astray, reveals God himself, who always rejoices in finding "the lost." Furthermore, in light of the statement, "Whoever has seen me has seen the Father" (John 14:9), we see that Jesus himself embodies the actions of God the Father, and therefore that the parable applies only in the second place to the heavenly Father.

2

The Structure of the Parable

The parable is structured as a diptych, a double picture, through which the behavior of both sons is intentionally thrown into contrast.[1] The introduction is followed by two main sections:[2]

1. Verses 12-24 (part A)
2. Verses 25-32 (part B)

The parable does not, therefore, have only one climax, but two: the banquet for the younger son and the conversation between the father and the elder son. It is on this second climax that the emphasis is laid and where the real intention of the evangelist is revealed.[3]

Introduction: The father and his two sons
Then Jesus said, "There was a man who had two sons. The younger of them said to his father, 'Father, give me the share of the property that will belong to me.' So he divided his property between them.

A. The younger son	**A'. The elder son**
1. Situation	
A few days later the younger son gathered all he had and traveled to a distant country, and there he squandered his property in dissolute living. When he had spent everything, a severe famine took place throughout that country, and he began to be in need. So he went and hired himself out to one of the citizens of that country, who sent him to his fields to feed the pigs. He would gladly have filled himself with the pods that the pigs were eating; and no one gave him anything.	Now his elder son was in the field; and when he came and approached the house, he heard music and dancing. He called one of the slaves and asked what was going on.
2. Realization	
But when he came to himself he said, 'How many of my father's hired hands have bread enough and to spare, but here I am dying of hunger! I will get up and go to my father, and I will say to him, "Father, I have sinned against heaven and before you; I am no longer worthy to be called your son; treat me like one of your hired hands."'	He replied, 'Your brother has come, and your father has killed the fatted calf, because he has got him back safe and sound.'
3. Reaction	
So he set off and went to his father.	Then he became angry and refused to go in.

B. The father and the younger son	B'. The father and the elder son
1. The father's initiative	
But while he was still far off, his father saw him and was filled with compassion; he ran and put his arms around him and kissed him.	His father came out and began to plead with him.
2. The sons' attitudes	
Then the son said to him, 'Father, I have sinned against heaven and before you; I am no longer worthy to be called your son.'	But he answered his father, 'Listen! For all these years I have been working like a slave for you, and I have never disobeyed your command; yet you have never given me even a young goat so that I might celebrate with my friends. But when this son of yours came back, who has devoured your property with prostitutes, you killed the fatted calf for him!'
3. The father's reaction	
But the father said to his slaves, 'Quickly, bring out a robe—the best one—and put it on him; put a ring on his finger and sandals on his feet. And get the fatted calf and kill it, and let us eat and celebrate; for this son of mine was dead and is alive again; he was lost and is found!' And they began to celebrate."	Then the father said to him, 'Son, you are always with me, and all that is mine is yours. But we had to celebrate and rejoice, because this brother of yours was dead and has come to life; he was lost and has been found.'"

3

Interpretation and Application of the Parable

The Son Leaves Home

$\mathcal{F}$rom the introduction we gather that the parable is about the relationship between a father and his two sons, and, by implication, about the relationship between the sons themselves.

Leaving aside speculation as to whether or not it was conceivable in Jesus' time to ask for a share of the inheritance and leave home,[1] given that it can hardly have been common, and was certainly far from being an expression of love, what strikes us initially is that the father gives willingly and without reproach. Actually, however, we later see that this behavior is perfectly in character: he behaves in the same way when the "prodigal" returns, and then, when the elder son refuses to go in and celebrate with the others, the father pleads with him and reassures him that everything in the house is his also. Again, he says this without reproach, even though he might at least have rebuked his son for his hardness and anger.

There have been some interesting interpretations of the sons' behavior toward their father. One suggests that it is really the father who is at fault: he had not shown his love for his sons openly enough, and, having made fundamental mistakes in their upbringing, is now reaping a harvest of their antagonism, anger, and discontent. Perhaps it goes without saying that even though this interpretation might reflect some of the causes of today's crisis in parent-child relationships, it far from fits the meaning of Jesus' parable.

But it is interesting that the Scripture avoids mentioning any of the younger son's "glaring sins." He confesses, "I have sinned against . . . you," but in this case they are not the usual sins that occur, however frequently, in normal families, such as anger, resentment, insults, or violence. His fundamental sin, or failing in life, consisted of breaking and trampling underfoot his relationship with his father and leaving for a "distant country." It is vital to understand this cardinal aspect of sin, which does not consist primarily in "breaking the law" but in trampling underfoot the loving relationship with God: leaving God, turning away from him, cutting adrift, and living life without him. The fact that we are often unable to perceive sin in any way other than "breaking the law" reflects our hardness of heart and our lack of understanding of sin as a breaching of the relationship with God; it attests to the fact that we do not have love for God. So it is tragic to understand our trespasses simply as a breaking of the law, as this leads only to soulless moralism and observing the letter of the law rather than the spirit.[2]

So the evangelist does not specify the sins the younger son committed in the far country; he merely points out that he "squandered his property in dissolute living," where the Greek word (adverb) *asōtōs* means foolishly, dissolutely, recklessly, profligately.[3] So we do not need to concern ourselves with his other sins because what was important had already been violated. (It is *possible* that he did not commit any other sins,[4] but simply enjoyed a life of freedom.)

On the spiritual level, the departure of the younger son cannot be understood only as a *flight from God.* He is also running away from the community, from the father's household, including his brother and the servants. His departure also symbolizes, therefore, a *flight from the church.* This form of escape—a rejection of the community—is also apparent in the grumbling Pharisees (and the elder brother) who chose not to participate in the banquet with "the early church gathered around the Lord."

Inner Disintegration

The younger son becomes estranged, a foreigner, a point that is driven home by his coming into contact with unclean animals. He has exchanged home for a foreign country, but his estrangement is not only external and visible. It is also internal, at the level of his identity, so that when he returns home he asks only to be made a servant—he does not feel like a son anymore! His identity has been distorted, tainted.

The estrangement of a human being from God truly leads to inner chaos, rupture, and disintegration. It creates inner pain, a weakening, a loss of identity, and eventually a general sickening and disgust at oneself, at everyone else, and ultimately at the whole of life.

The prophet Isaiah shows us, very graphically, an illuminating image of what goes on inside the fugitive:

I reared children and brought them up,
　　but they have rebelled against me.
The ox knows it owner,
　　and the donkey its master's crib;
But Israel does not know,
　　my people do not understand.
Ah, sinful nation,
　　people laden with iniquity,
offspring who do evil,
　　children who deal corruptly,
who have forsaken the LORD,
　　who have despised the Holy One of Israel,
　　who are utterly estranged!
Why do you seek further beatings?
　　Why do you continue to rebel?
The whole head is sick,
　　and the whole heart faint.
From the sole of the foot even to the head,
　　there is no soundness in it,
but bruises and sores
　　and bleeding wounds;
they have not been drained, or bound up,
　　or softened with oil. (Isa 1:2-6)

At the beginning, the younger son finds the father good only for fulfilling his needs, giving him what he wants. In spiritual terms, this is akin not to being interested in God himself, in "God as God," but only in "God as giver." More precisely, the concern is really only for his gifts, help, and blessings. Saint Teresa of Avila said, "God alone is enough," but we often have the sense that *for us God alone is not enough*, and it is not so much him we desire, but his gifts. (We can test this by asking ourselves what kind of prayers we usually pray—are they mainly or only prayers of petition?) At worst it is not only that God is not enough, but that we feel he is actually in the way of our happiness and freedom, and that it would be better to live without him, and a long way away.

Different Kinds of Flight from God

When we hear the parable of the Prodigal Son, we are tempted to identify not ourselves but "others" with the protagonist of the story, whether that be the younger or the elder son. Our concerns are more often than not with "other people," those disturbers of order and the cause of all our problems and the wretchedness of the world around us. Around a hundred years ago, the question, "What is wrong with the world?" appeared in an English newspaper, to which the author G. K. Chesterton sent the editor an unexpected answer, infused with typical English humor: "Dear Sirs, I am. Sincerely yours, G. K. Chesterton."[5]

In the spirit of Chesterton, we will leave behind for a moment the wretchedness of humankind and of those we love and will focus on the usual forms taken by *our own* flights from God. In practice there are various forms and degrees of "flight from the father's house," including not only that employed by the younger son but also that employed by his brother.

The flight of the younger son is characterized by a clear departure for a "distant country," a destination we can give various names: "self-realization," "virtual reality" (easily accessible today thanks to the media), "living in the past" (manifested as self-pity, feeling aggrieved, and a lack of forgiveness) or "living in the future" (careerism), and enjoying a life of freedom, a life without restraint.

The flight of the elder son is disguised, however. Such a person appears to live with God, but only for the sake of appearances. This is a more sophisticated form of flight from God. On the outside, the elder son stays at his father's house, but in his heart and his spirit he is really somewhere else. These kinds of people pray as if to God but in fact pray without God, without heart and without sincerity, not really needing the living God for their prayers. On the surface they live as Christians. They fulfill God's will, but with the attitude of a slave rather than that of a son or daughter. They feel the urge to do many things they would not normally do, either because they want to "get something" from God or because they are afraid of being punished.

Pursuing virtues, serving others, chasing after perfection or complete purity, striving for a "beautiful liturgy," going deeper in prayer, and making theological inquiries about "God's purposes"—these can all represent not only a flight from the living God but also a flight from our real self, a flight into a spiritual disguise, an artificial world of ideas, concepts, attitudes, and feelings.[6]

This form of flight is gradual and discreet. On the outside everything functions normally, giving the appearance of a pious and orderly life just like the elder son's: they pray and go to church, but only to fulfill their duty, and then they quickly leave as they do not feel at home there. Also, in private prayer, what matters is simply "getting it done" and fulfilling their religious duty. Prayer is tainted by a defense reflex, an inbuilt fear of the living God—anything to avoid getting too close to the burning fire of God's presence!

Even the reading of Scripture (if there is any) can be infected by this fear, and remains a purely intellectual exercise, thinking one's own thoughts rather than genuinely listening to the Word.

Furthermore, if we keep this defensive attitude toward God in our hearts, we can even turn God's word into a fortress to hide in, a fortress without the slightest chink through which grace might enter.[7] Such reading (or, during a service, hearing) is not really listening to what God wants to say to us personally—perhaps because, as the children of Israel knew very well, it is dangerous to hear the voice of the living God: "do not let God speak to us, or we will die" (Exod 20:19).

Finally, even our daily lives can be affected and pervaded by a kind of "practical atheism" in which we make decisions according to our own wishes and opinions, and where God is neither needed nor welcome. We do not have the courage to commit to God our work life, our conflicts at work or at home, our free time and hobbies, our holidays, our friendships. After all, "This is my business! What is wrong with me being in charge of all these things?"

But such a lifestyle is really a kind of spiritual schizophrenia. How can we call Jesus our Lord if he is our Lord only when we're in church, while everywhere else, and the rest of the time, it is we who are in charge of our lives? The verse, "This people honors me with their lips, / but their hearts are far from me" comes readily to mind for this kind of approach to life (Mark 7:6). Since conversion is not a once-for-all-time affair, a certain amount of practical atheism might always be there in our lives; however, what is important is to admit this duplicity, confess it, and follow the path of conversion—to have a change of heart.

Reaching Rock Bottom: "Shock Treatment"

Living a long way from home can be so difficult that we gradually begin to waste away. In the case of the younger son, his descent into destitution has three stages: first hunger, then having to earn a living feeding pigs (unclean animals), and, finally, envying even the pigs their food. He who had plenty now lacks even crumbs! He who enjoyed the dignity of sonship now lives with unclean animals and works as their unpaid servant!

He who was once completely free is now truly a slave—a swineherd, who would be happy to be given the pig feed to eat. Those who understand freedom as the radically arbitrary license to do just what they want and to have their own way are living in a lie, for by our very nature humans are a part of a shared existence and our freedom is shared freedom. Our very nature contains direction and norm, and becoming inwardly one with this direction and norm is what freedom is all about. A false autonomy thus leads to slavery: In the meantime history has taught us this all too clearly. For Jews the pig is an unclean animal, which means that the swineherd is the expression of a person's most extreme alienation and destitution. The totally free person has become a wretched slave.[8]

The consequences of leaving the father's house are now clear: emptiness, self-degradation, lacking even what the pigs have. It is a picture of utter humiliation: the son is worse off than the pigs! Why does he continue working for the landlord when he cannot even eat the pods the pigs are eating? This puts the finishing touch on the son's deep misery and humiliation. Degradation can sometimes go so far that it upsets the ability to assess a situation and act appropriately, upsets the ability to imagine that things could be different.

We too can find ourselves "with the swine" if we hold onto thoughts and intentions that we dare not say aloud. On his album *Unfit for Swine*, the Christian artist John Schlitt sings,

In the closet of my mind
I have thoughts unfit for swine
Secrets that I dare not tell
You know them well
'neath a veil of innocence
I disguise my decadence.[9]

It is good when a so-called free person becomes aware of his or her bonds and state of slavery and self-humiliation: "Know and see that it is evil and bitter / for you to forsake the LORD your God" (Jer 2:19). Saint Paul uses the same argument to affirm his readers and encourage them on their journey of new life in Christ: "So what advantage did you then get from the things of which you now are ashamed?" (Rom 6:21).

Remembering the terrible days "with the swine" can provide us with a healthy shock to the system. And if it provokes in us fresh courage to fight for what is good, we can ultimately, even of such a moment, declare "O happy fault," and the dark memories, in addition to filling our hearts with thankfulness for our salvation, can provide the antidote to falling even further.

Another kind of shock treatment lies in recognizing what God has done for us and noticing how we respond. Such treatment is very much in the spirit of the prophet Micah's words:

O my people, what have I done to you?
    In what have I wearied you? Answer me!
For I brought you up from the land of Egypt,
    and redeemed you from the house of slavery;
and I sent before you Moses, Aaron, and Miriam.
O my people, remember now what King Balak of Moab
        devised,
    what Balaam son of Beor answered him,

and what happened from Shittim to Gilgal,
    that you may know the saving acts of the LORD.
        (Mic 6:3-5)

But what difficulties has God caused us in the past? What wrong
has he done us? If we feel that he has caused us any injustice, we
can try to tell him, try to open this feeling of hurt or injustice
before him, and in this way hand it over to him. And if he has
not done anything wrong to us, why are we leaving him, sneak-
ing away from him?

Return to the Father

Fortunately, our story of the lost son does not end in catastrophe
but continues more promisingly:

> The prodigal son realizes that he is lost—that at home
> he was free and that his father's servants are freer than
> he now is, who had once considered himself completely
> free. "He went into himself," the Gospel says (Lk 15:17).
> As with the passage about the "far country," these words
> set the Church Fathers thinking philosophically: Living
> far away from home, from his origin, this man had also
> strayed far away from himself. He lived away from the
> truth of his existence.[10]

Eventually, it becomes impossible for the son to ignore the fact
that he is lost and dying. When we find ourselves scratching
around for our very existence, we reach a stage when we can no
longer deny what is happening and the reality of our miserable
state finally dawns on us.

The lost son finally does the sensible thing: he *goes into himself* ("came to himself," Luke 15:17) and decides to go home. He could have chosen a different solution such as *going somewhere else*, even further away, and trying his luck with a different landlord. But in fact he acts quite wisely for once, rather than continuing to brood over "what had happened, how and why" and losing himself in a never-ending labyrinth of his own self and his past.

We know very well how easy it is to give into the seductiveness of this kind of thought process. It can present a huge barrier to the journey of conversion, as *going into oneself* does not necessarily mean *going to the father*! By "going into ourselves," we can easily get bogged down in ourselves and our feelings of self-pity, bitterness, and despair—feelings that never solve anything. Saint Augustine describes the switch from "searching outside oneself" to "searching inside oneself": "For behold you were within me and I outside. And I sought you outside and in my unloveliness fell upon those lovely things that you made. You were with me and I was not with you."[11] In a similar way, the younger son was estranged from himself, just as he had in reality left for a far country. But now he is coming back to himself, and in "himself" he also finds the way back to the father and to regaining his dignity, the dignity of a son.[12] So the turning point comes at the height of the crisis. But in that case, if it is falling to the bottom that opens the younger son to grace, is it not better to sin? Paul addresses, and answers, this dilemma in his letter to the Romans: "What then are we to say? Should we continue in sin in order that grace may abound? By no means!" (6:1-2).

At first sight, the younger son looks like a "model penitent" precisely because of this "going into himself." It certainly appears that his conversion begins in his heart, that it is neither superficial nor affected. Furthermore, his inner conversion is confirmed by his physical return to the father and his words of confession: "I have sinned against heaven and before you" (Luke 15:21). Is this not, then, the best possible example of the ideal conversion process? Has this repentant sinner not been rightly offered as a perfect model in countless sermons?

Undoubtedly he has! On closer inspection, however, we see that his coming home was driven not so much by love for his father as by love of himself: "How many of my father's hired hands have bread enough and to spare, but here I am dying of hunger! I will get up and go to my father, and I will say to him, 'Father, I have sinned against heaven and before you'" (15:17, 18). The son is coming home, first and foremost, to save his own skin! He wants to start living; he is fed up with wasting away! He is coming back to his father in order to get what he wants, just as he did at the beginning of the story. Fundamentally, he has not changed at all. He is as calculated and self-centered as he ever was, the only difference being that now at least he wants to be close to his father. This represents a certain degree of progress in his thinking, but it is still quite far from being a complete shift to an attitude of love and selflessness.

Leaving aside discussion at the level of the parable for a while and moving to the more general, historical level, it is clear that Jesus was aware that all of the "younger sons," the tax collectors and sinners, followed him and stayed close to him because they felt at last they had space in which to breathe. They felt accepted; they felt God's love. But Jesus also knew that they were—for now—following him more for their own benefit than because of any feeling of love they might have had for him. He did not reproach them for this, however, as he knew that conversion is a gradual process.

Authentic Conversion and False Conversion

In some respects we may find ourselves in a more difficult position today than that of the tax collectors and sinners. The endless appeals to conversion and repetitive confessions and pleas for forgiveness can have the opposite of the desired effect: they can sear our consciences and blur our vision so that we end up not knowing *what* to repent of and *how* to repent of it.

What Do We Repent Of?

We see our life as if through a "keyhole": we see only fragments; we fail to notice many things and are not aware of the wider context. We need someone to open the door for us and help us to see what is hidden inside, in the house of our heart, and that "someone" is God himself. The one who says, "I am standing at the door, knocking" (Rev 3:20) is waiting for our invitation. He opens the door and shows us all of the dirt, dust, and cobwebs that are still in our house, in our cellar. But he opens the door only gradually—if he opened it all in one go, we would probably fall into despair at ourselves.

Changing the image slightly, if our door is always open by the same amount, we always see the same cobwebs, the same sins. We come to confession with chronically repetitive sins and it seems like we are going round and round in circles. The will is there, but there is no significant change, either for better or for worse.

A few years ago, one winter, I was staying in the Šumava National Park. When I needed to leave, I started the car and put it into reverse . . . but the wheels just spun in the snow. Naturally I tried everything possible: I revved the engine, stopped, revved again, all the time turning the steering wheel left and right. In despair I tried increasing the revs even more, but to no avail. The engine roared but the car stayed put. Then suddenly a kindly man appeared out of nowhere, leaned on the hood, and with very little effort pushed the car out of the ruts I had created. So it didn't really take much. . . .

We experience something like this on the spiritual level when we strive with all our might for conversion and a deep spiritual life but eventually realize we are getting absolutely nowhere. There is a lot of noise but no movement, and what we really need is "someone" to give us a gentle push.

Clearly this "mysterious helper" is, first and foremost, God, who sometimes acts or calls us directly, and at other times acts through other people or events. We should beware, therefore, of rejecting such a helper by saying, "I can manage by myself, thank you." I might not say it aloud; I might just try harder to live "my own life my own way."[13] Yet surely this is perfectly acceptable, isn't it? We "mature Christians" know exactly what is and is not sin, are quite willing to "better ourselves," and know all about the mistakes we make and certainly want to correct them. "Spinning the wheels" without getting anywhere despite our best efforts provides us, however, with an important lesson in humility, teaching us that we cannot manage on our own and that we need a push from someone else. We need the courage to say, "Lord, show me my mistakes and what their roots are, but let it be *you* who helps me to change."

How does God answer such a prayer? Sometimes he does it through a "word." Whether this word comes to us from another person, or the Bible, or the depths of our hearts, or perhaps a concrete event, it strikes us, convicts us, and pierces our hearts,[14] just as it did for those who heard Peter's sermon on the day of Pentecost. They did not simply give an emotional response but experienced a deep and genuine conversion that manifested itself in a desire and a willingness to change: "Brothers, what should we do?" (Acts 2:37).

But God's word "pierces" us in different ways from a mere human word: the former sets us free by the truth, the latter knocks us down and strikes us dead. The sword of God's word cuts the chains of lies and self-deceit and sets us free, while the sword of a human word just cuts us in two! The writer to the Hebrews puts it like this: "Indeed, the word of God is living and active, sharper than any two-edged sword, piercing until it divides soul from spirit, joints from marrow; it is able to judge the thoughts and intentions of the heart. And before him no creature is hidden, but all are naked and laid bare to the eyes of the one to whom we must render an account" (Heb 4:12-13).

What is our reaction when we read these words? Are we horrified? afraid? Are we desperate to "escape God's word"? These reactions are predictable and perfectly natural, which is why the writer adds in the very next verse, "Since, then, we have a great high priest who has passed through the heavens, Jesus, the Son of God, let us hold fast to our confession. For we do not have a high priest who is unable to sympathize with our weaknesses, but we have one who in every respect has been tested as we are, yet without sin" (Heb 4:14-15).

God understands our weakness, is compassionate with us, wants to save us, and his words of conviction spring *from the depths of his empathy*. Christ is not against us; he is for us. He is a merciful and compassionate Lord, which is why we can fully and fearlessly expose ourselves to his words. God does not convict us in the same way as our neurotic conscience, or like someone who is not led by Christ's spirit, and especially not like the Evil One! The Holy Spirit admonishes, strengthens, and liberates; the admonishment of "others" discourages us and throws us into despair.

At this point we could perhaps lighten things up a little with a story: A certain priest had been trying for years to convert his parishioners, but to no avail. At one point during one of his sermons he turned away to blow his nose. After the service, one of the congregation came to talk to him and said that the sermon was magnificent and she had gained much from it. The priest asked what exactly had spoken to her so much, and she replied, "The way you blew your nose so loudly reminded me of the angels blowing their trumpets at the Last Judgment, and that really woke me up and I was converted on the spot!"

It is in just this kind of gentle, unobtrusive, but effective way that God admonishes us. It is the admonishment that comes through parables, the way we know it from Jesus' sermons. Moreover, admonishment from the Spirit is always concrete rather than nebulous: if we have only a vague "guilty conscience" without any clear sense of what the actual failure was, then it was not God's admonishment!

Finally, there is nothing better than to pray to the Spirit, asking for a revelation of the dark, hidden chambers of our hearts; to expose ourselves to God's word with our hearts laid open and to let ourselves be admonished, and not only when we are preparing for confession! God wants us to live, not to die, even when we're in sin! This may sound unbelievable, but it is the truth of the gospel that Jesus proclaimed: "I came not to judge the world, but to save the world" (John 12:47).

How Do We Repent?

We have all, during confession, heard the priest's appeal to us: "Make your act of contrition!" But is bringing about repentance a simple and natural thing to do? How can we make it happen? We may sometimes realize that our hard-won repentance is actually quite superficial. We may even question whether we have any real remorse at all when we commit "the same old sins" time and again, even after confessing them.

The younger son is probably more like us than we think he is. Not just in his extravagant, easygoing lifestyle, but in the kind of repentance he showed (if we can call it repentance). We have seen that he was full of self-pity and self-love, and that his return home was driven by a desire for self-preservation, but this is often how it is with us as well! What is the main reason for our going to confession? To ease our conscience? To find inner peace? If we look closely, this is exactly what motivated the younger son. He wanted some fresh air; he wanted to start living again! Sometimes we come back to God for our own sake rather than to mend our broken relationship with him (which we might not even realize is broken).

My "remorse" can stem from other factors as well, such as disappointment with myself: to sin means to fail, which means I fall short of the ideal image I have of myself. My remorse can simply be because I failed to show myself in a good light, that I behaved embarrassingly. Such self-pity then prompts me to correct and improve myself, and my prayers of penitence and my trips to confession simply become tools for achieving that improvement. However, regrettably, even in the case of "mature Christians," this attempt at change, at conversion, can be driven by a desire to improve my own *image*, which has suffered from sin, and all I really want is to be able to look myself in the mirror with pride and self-satisfaction!

For example, my sorrow at having been, say, unreasonably angry can have various causes: I have embarrassed myself in front of others and now look like an impossible Mr. Angry who completely lacks self-control; or I unjustly walked all over the other person; or at that moment there was no space in my heart for Christ's gentleness and love.

What does God think of our worn-out attempts at conversion? Do we think conversion is all about our own self-improvement? Or is it not, rather, about a new and deeper relationship with God and with others (including ourselves)—in other words, about love? If this is indeed the case, God probably leaves us to fail on our journey of (false) conversion, time and again, so that we will eventually realize that what we are attempting is a "Sisyphean" ascent, and furthermore that we are heading for the wrong summit: not God, but our own ego!

How Can We Truly Repent?

It all starts with being remorseful over our inability to truly repent—to admit that our repentance is selfish, self-centered, and has ulterior motives. This remorse will then lead us to desire and seek a new kind of repentance, which is repentance that comes from love. Furthermore, this remorse is already a fruit of the operation of God's love—it is a consequence of knowing that what matters is a relationship rather than self-realization. Being aware of this inspires in us a desire for "true repentance," which is a gift, as the seventh-century ascetic Isaac the Syrian wrote:

> The one who is conscious of his sins is greater than the one who profits the world by the sight of his countenance. The

one who sighs over his soul for but one hour is greater than the one who raises the dead by his prayers while dwelling among human beings. The one who is deemed worthy to see himself is greater than the one who is deemed worthy to see angels.[15]

If we ever met someone who had seen an angel, or raised the dead, we would think this person is exceptionally blessed. But Saint Isaac does not hesitate to claim that the one who "sighs over his soul" and sees himself as he truly is, is even more blessed! So true repentance is indeed a great and precious gift— but it is just that, a gift, and not the fruit of human endeavor.

Elsewhere, Saint Isaac compares the penitent to the martyr, as both experience rebirth, purification, new life, and a fresh breath of God's Spirit. True repentance is not about darkness and depression. Yes, it means pain, but pain suffused with the joy of God's forgiving love. The early fathers, among them Saint Jerome, spoke of the waters of baptism and the tears of repentance as two kinds of purifying water, each of which purifies our hearts and brings us new life.

Coming face-to-face with the gift of "repentance born of love," it is impossible not to desire and ask for such a precious gift. Saint Francis could spend all night crying because "love was not loved," either by him or by the rest of the world. He was not crying because he felt he had wasted a large part of his life, but because he realized how ungrateful and unfaithful he had been toward this Love: the "little poor man" from Assisi cried out of love.

Long before Francis, Saint Peter had a similar experience: "The Lord turned and looked at Peter. Then Peter remembered the word of the Lord, how he had said to him, 'Before the cock crows today, you will deny me three times.' And he went out and wept bitterly" (Luke 22:61-62). Notice, however, what it was that caused Peter's tears: it was not seeing his own fickleness and unfaithfulness; it was the loving look that Jesus gave him. It was Peter's seeing the way Jesus looked at him that caused his tears of repentance!

We see something very different—albeit quite similar on the surface—in the case of Judas (see Matt 26:69–27:10). He too regrets his behavior toward Jesus, but his remorse is very different from Peter's, as is implied by the use of the Greek word *metamelomai*, which means simply "to regret" and is used in the case of Judas rather than *metanoeō*, which means "to change one's mind, to convert." We can also see the difference between these two kinds of repentance by their "fruit": in Peter's case the fruit of repentance is seen in his coming back to Christ, back to a new and deeper relationship of love; with Judas it is more like self-pity, which, even though he had the same chance as Peter to return to Christ, eventually leads him to despair and self-destruction.

So who lives in us: Peter or Judas? Is our repentance more like that of Judas, being annoyed that we failed to cope and messed up? Or that of Peter, bringing us back to Christ (see John 21:15-19)? We continually need to discern whether we are driven by the penitence of Peter or that of Judas. The first leads to Christ; the second plunges us into depression and a sense of failure, starting with self-condemnation and telling ourselves off, and leading to self-rejection, self-punishment, and even self-destruction. It looks like repentance but descends into self-hatred and a lack of faith in God's forgiveness.

Some years ago a simple sentence from the book of Jeremiah spoke to my heart: "Turn thou me, and I shall be turned" (31:18; author's preferred translation[16]). I repeated these words to myself for several weeks and felt some very positive effects, which should not, of course, have been a surprise as God hears the prayers of the helpless person who relies on him and confesses one's powerlessness and inability to change or to truly convert!

This simple plea ("Turn thou me . . .") is interesting in that it exposes the complete powerlessness of the sinner who is "on the way of conversion." It is a plea for true conversion, sincere repentance, and a transformation of one's life. Notice that Israel utters the plea immediately after expressing the painful experience of having failed to return to God by their own efforts: "You disciplined me, . . . like a calf untrained"[17] (Jer 31:18). The prayer includes a request to recognize the hidden sins, as these are also included in the overall process of conversion. And, most importantly, God answers the prayer of penitence offered by "the helpless" by his promise: "I will surely have mercy on him, / says the LORD" (31:20).

Zechariah also highlights the fact that true repentance is a gift from God:

> And I will pour out a spirit of compassion and supplication on the house of David and the inhabitants of Jerusalem, so that, when they look on the one whom they have pierced, they shall mourn for him, as one mourns for an only child, and weep bitterly over him, as one weeps over a firstborn. (Zech 12:10)

It is God who pours out the spirit of supplication, and thanks to this gift "the house of David" look to the Lord and not to themselves—their cry is for God's sake, not their own. A further example is provided by the anonymous "sinful" woman who comes to Jesus and wets his feet with her tears (Luke 7:36-50). She fixes her gaze on Christ; *she looks up at him.* The tears are not superficial; they are tears of love, a profound display of her love for him. The Lord himself affirms this when he says, "her sins, which were many, have been forgiven; hence she has shown great love" (Luke 7:47).

True contrition is a blessing that can be received only as a gift, but it is also true that we can open ourselves up to it and take hold of it, guided by Psalm 51, the most famous prayer of penitence: "Have mercy on me, O God, / according to your steadfast love; / according to your abundant mercy."

Christ as "Mother"

"So he set off and went to his father. But while he was still far off, his father saw him and was filled with compassion [he was moved to his innermost being]; he ran and put his arms around him and kissed him" (Luke 15:20). Notice that the father was moved to his innermost being. The word *esplagchnisthē*, related to *splagchna*, can also mean "mother's womb" or "entrails" or "seat of motherly affections." The expression could therefore be translated as "moved to his guts," with the associated nuance of a mother's heart or "innards," or the seat of her affection for her child.

So the father is clearly very far from feeling indifferent or impassive when he sees his wretched son; on the contrary, he is moved to the very depths of his being. Compassion, true compassion, springs from the depths of his heart and manifests itself in the visible acts of hugging, kissing, and showering with gifts.

It does not begin with the outward acts but begins with being inwardly moved; it does not come from outside but inside, from the heart, from the most profound depths of the heart, from the seat of "motherly" affection.

That is why purely external acts of compassion are empty, worthless: "If I give away all my possessions . . . but do not have love, I gain nothing," writes the apostle Paul (1 Cor 13:3). Acts of compassion should spring from the depths of the heart like gushing water springs from the depths of the earth. We find the same word for compassion in the parable of the Good Samaritan: "and when he saw him, he was moved with pity [compassion]" (Luke 10:33). The concrete expressions of the Samaritan's compassion sprang from this inner "movement." In the same way, earlier in the gospel, Christ was "moved" in his heart and "had compassion" on the widow of Nain when he saw her weeping (Luke 7:13); his moved heart led him to a concrete act of compassion, in this case the miracle of raising the widow's son.

But perhaps the most significant occurrence of the same word is found at the very beginning of Luke's gospel, in the song of Zechariah: "*From the heart of compassionate love* he will dawn on us, the One who comes from on high" (Luke 1:78; author's translation). Christ is a gift springing from the Father's very womb, from the depths of his compassion, in the same way that a child comes into the world from its mother's womb.

Compassion Restores Dignity

Moved in his heart, the father runs to his son, embraces him, and kisses him. Remember that this is the wayward son who had left his father in order to live life on his own, who had asked for his share of the inheritance while his father was still alive and in so doing had shown he did not care about him and considered him already dead. The son was concerned more about himself than the father, but the father behaves toward the son quite differently: he is deeply concerned. Moved in his heart, he runs to his son and hugs and kisses him as if nothing had happened, as if the son had nothing to apologize for.

The father's compassionate heart sees first and foremost a man he loves, not a "sinner," and so, wanting to meet this loved one *face-to-face*, he hugs and kisses him. Here God is not taking the role of policeman or judge; his first concern is for the person rather than the sin or the misdeeds.

How do we perceive God and his relationship with us when the qualms of conscience descend upon us, when we find ourselves "in sin," or when we are at confession? In *that moment* do we perceive God as the merciful father? Or as the policeman to whom we need to give account for our misdeeds? Perhaps we look on him as someone who sees mainly our faults and so withdraws from us and rejects us. It would be understandable if we imagined God's attitude toward us, "the sinner," like this, as this is often our attitude toward "sinful" others whose faults are what we mostly see. But fortunately for us God says, "I am God and no mortal" (Hos 11:9).

What really shows how we see God in the moments we become aware of our sin is the *nature* of our prayer. If we truly know God's mercy, our prayer for forgiveness already anticipates thanksgiving as we have real *inner certainty* of God's mercy and therefore of God's forgiveness.

God's Search

A profound comment from Henri Nouwen relates perfectly to the scene in the parable where the father meets the younger son. Nouwen suggests that God wants to find us "as much as, if not more than, [we] want to find God."[18] However great—or small—our desire for God's presence, it is this certainty over God's passionate desire that gives us strength. But why does God "passionately search for us"? It is because he is, as Saint Therese of Lisieux wrote, "the divine prisoner of love,"[19] and bound with this love he binds his prodigal children to himself "with cords of human kindness, / with bands of love" (Hos 11:4). Furthermore, we hear in Isaiah: "Can a woman forget her nursing child, / or show no compassion for the child of her womb? / Even these may forget, / yet I will not forget you" (Isa 49:15).

These texts show us the real maternal character of our God: patience with the sinner, compassion, immeasurable kindness, and forgiveness without reproach. God is indeed both father and mother, or, more accurately, has both motherly and fatherly characteristics. We often think of kindness and forgiveness as signs of weakness and passivity. The prophet Hosea, however, suggests otherwise: "My heart recoils within me; / my compassion grows warm and tender. / I will not execute my fierce anger; / I will not again destroy Ephraim; / for I am God and no mortal, / the Holy One in your midst, / and I will not come in wrath" (Hos 11:8-9). The anthropomorphic[20] phrase "My heart recoils within me" is intended to portray the extent of God's passionate love for mankind. God's compassion springs from a passionate vitality; it is an unstoppable torrent of love issuing from the womb of the Trinity. Such a torrent will irresistibly sweep away our sins, just as, in similar vein, Isaac the Syrian writes, "As a handful of sand thrown into the ocean, so are the sins of all flesh as compared with the mind of God. Just as a strongly flowing fountain is not blocked up by a handful of earth, so the compassion of the Creator is not overcome by the wickedness of his creatures."[21] Similarly, Silouan of Mount Athos proclaims, "Many people think to themselves, 'I have sinned much in life' . . . But they forget that in God's sight all their sins are as drops of water in the sea."[22]

Prodigal Love

A compassionate heart also manifests itself in *weakness* for the other. This "weakness" can be seen in the father's actions: despite all of the conventions—such as those relating to his position in society as a noble patriarch—he runs to meet his son, embraces him, and kisses him, even before the son has a chance to apologize! It is as if *he* was reconciling with the *son*, rather than the other way around! In his words to his son, the father makes no mention of any sin. He does not say, "What have you done to me?" The important thing is that his son is back. He is not interested in his son's confession; it is the son himself who is more important![23] And his son is here—he has come back!

Compassion desires, first and foremost, meeting the other; showing love with a tangible gift comes second. So first come the father's embrace and kiss, and then come the material gifts. Giving is a consequence of *a personal encounter*. The warm embrace therefore precedes the father's "prodigal" giving, not of a simple cloak, but the most beautiful robe; not only giving the son his dignity back, but giving him a ring, a symbol of power (see Gen 41:42; Esth 3:10; 8:8-10). Sandals are not enough, so he gives him the finest shoes (*hypodēmata*), those usually worn by prominent people on special occasions; a kid won't do, so they kill the fatted calf, kept for a special feast, not of simple food, but a banquet only the rich could afford. And as if that weren't enough, the father arranges for music and dancing. The father's *compassion knows no limits*—he is truly prodigal in his love. But he does not forget the elder son: after generously giving his younger son all he has, he reassures the elder son that everything he owns is his also.

God loves without measure and without limit. He has compassion on those who find themselves in material and spiritual poverty (the younger son) as well as those experiencing inner poverty (the elder son). His wild expressions of compassion flow from the dictates of love toward particular individuals, not simply "people in general," just as the evangelist tells us that the father's heart was moved when he saw his son on his way home. The father *is not indifferent* to his children's needs. His generosity is conditioned neither by good deeds (the younger son was actually full of misdeeds) nor by the right kind of repentance (his son had failed in this too as his loving intentions toward the father were far from perfect, coming home as he did mainly for his own survival [vv. 15, 17]). Despite this, the father does not cast him out reproachfully; he does not send him away empty-handed. On the contrary, he gives to him in full measure, not only material gifts, but lavishing upon him his fatherly (and motherly) affection, accepting him unconditionally.

Whereas both of the sons are calculating and scheming in their attempts to get something out of their father's estate, the father acts without calculation and out of pure love, as we can see when he gives his sons their share of the estate at the beginning of the story, and especially from how he behaves when the prodigal son returns. Without needing a reason to do so, he gives the son what he does not deserve, not because the son showed sincere remorse (his words were, on the contrary, insincere), but because he himself is merciful. The image of the father running toward his younger son and kissing him even before he is able to deliver his ready-made speech is encapsulated in Paul's words to the Romans, "But God proves his love for us in that while we still were sinners Christ died for us" (Rom 5:8), and in the First Letter of John, "In this is love, not that we loved God but that he loved us and sent his Son to be the atoning sacrifice for our sins" (1 John 4:10).

Saint Therese of Lisieux also had this certainty: "Even though I had on my conscience all the sins that can be committed I would go, my heart broken with sorrow, and throw myself into Jesus' arms."[24] We too, in just such a situation, can throw ourselves at Jesus with the confidence that he will be the first to run toward us and lovingly embrace us.

Mercy, then, is not conditioned by the *deeds* of the other: it comes first, it takes the initiative. It does not think in terms of "if" (I will be kind *if* you . . . , *when* you . . .), but rather "even though" (I will be merciful to you *even though* you do not deserve it). This is affirmed in Luke 6:35, where the father shows his mercy by being "kind to the ungrateful and the wicked." And what is the measure of his kindness? It is a "good measure, pressed down, shaken together, running over" (Luke 6:38), just as we see in our parable.

The father is also a "Good Samaritan" (Luke 10:33-35). In our text, as in the parable of the Good Samaritan, there are seven expressions of mercy. The number seven is the number of fullness or completion, so the Father-Good-Samaritan does everything for his son! The father and the Samaritan both take care of and look after someone in need, and both of them continue their care through their servants.

So we can justifiably call our parable the Merciful Father. We could go further, however, and describe the father not simply as merciful but as *prodigal*, as he acts more than mercifully. Forgiving the younger son and giving him all he needs would certainly be merciful, but he goes much further, surpassing the bounds of mercy and giving his son "good measure . . . running over." The prodigal in the story is therefore the father rather than the younger son, although each is prodigal in his own way: the son squanders on himself, the father on the other; the son out of egoism, the father out of compassion; the son indulges *himself* without restraint, but the father indulges the *other* boundlessly, without limit—he is merciful without limit, and he is prodigal in love.

Excessive Love

But why does the father in the parable, in other words Christ, give "good measure . . . running over"? Why? Because he is simply like that, and this also holds true for God: "I love because I love."[25] There is no other reason for his merciful behavior than this: he is merciful because he is merciful; his mercy springs from a merciful heart. God is merciful not because he sees people in need, but because loving them, blessing them, is a requirement of his love.

This is why, with Elizabeth of the Trinity, we dare to talk about God's *excessive love*.[26] We may be ready to admit that God loves us, but that he loves us *excessively*—who among us could imagine such a love? And what if we receive this *excessive* love? Will it make us feel elated? Isn't it just another "catchy tune"? Is there any proof that this kind of love actually exists? Yes, absolutely! It is here in our parable, in the father's boundless love, love we do not see every day, extravagant love that completely transcends our ideas of goodness and forgiveness, because yes, Jesus' love is extravagant, excessive, and beyond comprehension.

In his letter to the Ephesians, Paul says that not only is God "rich in mercy" but that he loved us "out of [his] great love" (Eph 2:4), and it was this verse that inspired Elizabeth of the Trinity to meditate upon "excessive love." The verses that follow are yet more eloquent, and speak of the immeasurable or all-transcending riches of God's grace: "that in the ages to come he might show the immeasurable riches of his grace in kindness toward us in Christ Jesus" (Eph 2:7). In one of her letters, filled with the deep revelation of God's love as a limitless ocean, Elizabeth urges her mother superior, "allow yourself to be loved even more,"[27] meaning "accept that God loves you more than you have so far been able to understand or experience, and throw yourself into this ocean"—like the younger son in the parable who allowed himself to be embraced by his father.

Danish philosopher Søren Kierkegaard said that what matters is not whether God "is" but whether he "is love."[28] We could go further than this already profound truth and say it does not matter so much that we believe in God but that we believe in God-Love and truly live out of this love, and, furthermore, that we learn to live out of his *excessive* love. Elizabeth of the Trinity offers us a further clue as to how we can do this:

"Walk in Jesus Christ the Lord," [the Apostle tells me,] "rooted and built up in Him, and confirmed in the faith, . . . abounding in Him in thanksgiving."

"Walk in Jesus Christ" appears to me to mean to go out from self, to lose sight of, to forsake self, that we may enter more deeply into Him every moment—enter so profoundly as to be "rooted" in Him, and that we may boldly challenge all events with the defiant cry: "Who, then, shall separate us from the love of Christ?" When the soul is so deeply fixed in Him as to be rooted in Him, the divine sap flows freely through it and destroys whatever in its life was trivial, imperfect, unspiritual: "Mortality is absorbed in life."[29]

Being Thankful for God's Love

It struck me recently that we have a real treasure tucked away in the second eucharistic prayer in the Mass for children, where we repeat a number of times, "Thank you, O God, for your love." I realized that to thank in this way is to focus on what is most important. Although it is of course right to give thanks for all that is good around us, to thank God *for his love* means to see and accept the most precious gift, the Gift of gifts. Jesus spoke about this to the Samaritan woman at the well: "If you knew the gift of God, and who it is that is saying to you, 'Give me a drink,' you would have asked him . . ." (John 4:10). God's love is our atmosphere, in which we live and without which we cannot breathe. To live in this love means to believe that it is as real as the air that surrounds us from morning till evening. The testimony of Elizabeth of the Trinity, who practiced this way of life, seeks to further encourage and convince us: "I feel His love descending on my soul! It is like an ocean into which I plunge and lose myself."[30]

But if truth be known, we do not always feel the warmth of God's presence. Sometimes trials and tribulations and feelings of anxiety and despondency press into our lives. In these moments, and others that may be yet more difficult, moments that are laced with pain and failure, we need to "believe in love" (see 1 John 4:16). Even during the hard times we can express our faith in those simple words of thanks: "Thank you, O God, for your love." And through all the twists and turns of life's journey, interwoven with light and shadows, we can take to heart the words of the well-known theologian Hans Urs von Balthasar: "The only infinite thing, O Christ, is your love."[31]

Creative Forgiveness

But is it somewhat meaningless to speak of God's *excessive* love? Is it just Christian sentimentalism? Absolutely not! If we truly experience the breadth and length, the height and depth of Christ's love that surpasses all knowledge (Eph 3:18-19), we simply cannot but be changed! Knowing this—and "knowing" it in the biblical sense of the word, wherein knowledge affects the entire person, not merely the intellect—brings complete transformation.

In our story, the younger son receives not only forgiveness but a new robe, a ring, and sandals. Suddenly he is a new person with new dignity. He must surely have been surprised by his father's reaction: he had only asked, and timidly at that, to be made his servant, but the father has now completely restored his dignity. The Father's forgiveness is "creative" not only because it surpasses commonly held notions of reconciliation with a wayward son, but because it creates something new, a new person. Hence God's forgiveness is a creative act in the proper meaning of the word.

It is interesting to note how "salvation"—or "rescue"—is described here. The father in the parable does not actually say the words "I forgive you," which further suggests that Jesus is more concerned about the person than the sin. Rather, he shows his son his affection and the warmth of his love—love that gives, prodigally. We might have expected the father to give the son a speech, but he simply gives, just as he had before the son departed. His gestures of affection are no less expressive than a speech, however. In fact, they offer more than words, and verbal assurance would in any case have been superfluous. To accept forgiveness, then, does not mean simply "to turn over a new leaf," but to accept transformation, and this transformation is, moreover, already included in the gift of forgiveness itself! It is expressed implicitly in our story, but explicitly by the prophet Ezekiel: "I will sprinkle clean water upon you, and you shall be clean from all your uncleannesses, and from all your idols I will cleanse you. A new heart I will give you, and a new spirit I will put within you; and I will remove from your body the heart of stone and give you a heart of flesh. I will put my spirit within you, and make you follow my statutes and be careful to observe my ordinances" (Ezek 36:25-27).

So forgiveness is a *new creation*! It is the gift of a new heart, and the heart is not only the center of our emotions but the center of the whole of our inner life, the place where we experience relationships, our consciousness, our conscience, our reason, and our will. Ezekiel is prophesying about a heart transplant: God's forgiveness will cause an exchange, replacing the old heart, the heart of stone, insensitive and unable to hear

God and his invitations, with a new and authentically human heart, responsive to God's call and conforming to God's original creative intent.

To ask for forgiveness is to ask for a new heart, without which it is in fact impossible to accept forgiveness. The psalmist affirms this: "Let me hear joy and gladness; / let the bones that you have crushed rejoice. / Hide your face from my sins, / and blot out all my iniquities. / Create in me a clean heart, O God, / and put a new and right spirit within me. / Do not cast me away from your presence, / and do not take your holy spirit from me" (Ps 51:8-11).

Real prayer for forgiveness includes a plea for an experience of the joy of God's presence, and a plea for a new heart, for new and transformed relationships, as the human heart is the center of the whole person, where relationships are experienced and lived.

We have all, on occasion, experienced the transforming power of forgiveness, whether through the sacrament of confession or through a prayer of genuine penitence. We need to be conscious of the fact that reconciliation with God is not a trivial matter; it is not only a clearing of debts but is a creative act. Dietrich Bonhoeffer said that this is not "cheap grace."[32] What does he mean by this? Can grace be cheap, or costly? Is grace not always free? Of course, but Bonhoeffer means something else. Cheap grace is grace that leaves us indifferent or halfhearted: "So, I've received forgiveness—what's so special about that? I know this very well—I have known it for years!" Costly grace, on the other hand, is grace that is dear to us because we feel how dearly it is paid for by the one who offers it. And that is why it attracts, motivates, and mobilizes a person into a new lifestyle. If we have received a new robe, a sign of the renewed dignity of

sonship, then we should live as sons of God and not return to
the pigs: noblesse oblige!

To allow myself to be forgiven means to leave the past behind and start again: "So if anyone is in Christ, there is a new
creation: everything old has passed away; see, everything has
become new!" (2 Cor 5:17). I can let Jesus' words, "Go your
way, and from now on do not sin again" (John 8:11), help me
consciously adopt a new lifestyle: after every confession I can
let the words resonate in my heart, for they are words of power,
the power of Jesus. Another Bible passage that will open my eyes
to the costly grace of forgiveness is Psalm 103, which I can also
usefully recite after confession. The opening verses of the psalm
confirm once again how closely forgiveness is connected with
inner transformation:

> Bless the LORD, O my soul;
>   and all that is within me,
>   bless his holy name.
> Bless the LORD, O my soul,
>   and do not forget all his benefits—
> who forgives all your iniquity,
>   who heals all your diseases,
> who redeems your life from the Pit,
>   who crowns you with steadfast love and mercy,
> who satisfies you with good as long as you live
>   so that your youth is renewed like the eagles.
>   (Ps 103:1-5)

But we need not use words alone, even biblical words: the father
welcomed his son back with gifts and a banquet, not simply with
words. I know some people who celebrate reconciliation with

a meal and a symbolic toast; if we throw celebration banquets after baptisms and weddings, why not indeed do the same after the sacrament of reconciliation?

The Elder Son: The "Hardened Self-Righteous"

Luke's parable is a little like a film that has two protagonists: the first is a rather bumbling and unfortunate but in the end likeable character who is able to admit his mistakes; the second is the seemingly more clean-cut, naturally "good" character who is gradually revealed as uncompassionate and mean. So far we have concentrated on the first character, the younger son; it is now time to shift our attention to the second, his elder brother.

The banquet in honor of the younger son does not happen on a special holiday but on a normal working day, which we know from the fact that the elder son "was in the field" (15:25). The surprise nature of the feast is thus all the more apparent, so perhaps we can understand when the elder son does not immediately realize what is happening. He calls one of the servants and asks him what is going on, and the servant replies, "Your brother has come, and your father has killed the fatted calf, because he has got him back safe and sound" (v. 27). This explanation is not, however, completely accurate. What the father is rejoicing over is the restored relationship: the son was lost, he was dead,[33] but is now found again.

So the elder son's angry reaction to the servant's news is quite understandable. He may have been able to tolerate his father's compassion, but what he cannot accept is his father's giving without measure and without reason. This is what he complains so bitterly about to his father a few minutes later—"you have never given me even a young goat" (v. 29)—even though, in the son's mind, there could have been any number of reasons for the father to have done this as he had served him dutifully all his life.

To the elder son, the father's "prodigality" is truly shocking, but the father gives because he wants to give, because he is good—no other reason is needed. We see a piece of equally "shocking" behavior in the parable of the Laborers in the Vineyard (Matt 20:1-16). It was the vineyard owner's giving without measure, giving in a way that lacked, or exceeded, any kind of human logic, that the most diligent laborers grumbled about: "These last worked only one hour, and you have made them equal to us who have borne the burden of the day and the scorching heat" (Matt 20:12). They grumble only because their master is good (see v. 15). How strange! God's goodness gives rise to anger and resentment among the "righteous." Instead of joy there is sadness, envy, and anger. Where did it go wrong? The answer is clear—the wrong is in humankind, as the vineyard owner suggests: "Or are you envious because I am generous?" (Matt 20:15).

But this serious flaw is masked by an apparent sense of justice: a life full of hard work, as in the case of the elder brother (and the workers hired in the first hour), looks highly respectful compared to the murky past (or the short period of service) of others. But it is this very obedience, which is more like the obedience of a slave than that of a "son," that later generates bitterness and dissatisfaction as it gained them little profit:[34]

> After all, what Jesus says about the older brother is aimed not simply at Israel . . . but at the specific temptation of the righteous, of those who are *"en règle,"* at rights with God, as Grelot puts it (p. 229). . . . For them, more than anything else God is Law; they see themselves in a juridical relation-

ship with God and in that relationship they are at rights with him. But God is greater: They need to convert from the Law-God to the greater God, the God of love. This will not mean giving up their obedience, but rather that this obedience will flow from deeper wellsprings and will therefore be bigger, more open, and purer, but above all more humble.[35]

Sometimes we may feel like the clean-cut elder son, who stays with the father and dutifully serves him. But this "staying" may be deceptive: we may be *beside the father* but at the same time not *with him* at all. We can seem like "good Christians" but actually be more like the Christians from Laodicea, who also believed they were, like the elder son, without fault, but whom Christ admonishes vehemently:

> I know your works; you are neither cold nor hot. I wish that you were either cold or hot. So, because you are lukewarm, and neither cold nor hot, I am about to spit you out of my mouth. For you say, "I am rich, I have prospered, and I need nothing." You do not realize that you are wretched, pitiable, poor, blind, and naked. Therefore I counsel you to buy from me gold refined by fire so that you may be rich; and white robes to clothe you and to keep the shame of your nakedness from being seen; and salve to anoint your eyes so that you may see. I reprove and discipline those whom I love. Be earnest, therefore, and repent. (Rev 3:15-19)

The elder son was also a little like Paul the Pharisee, who according to his own words exceeded other Jews in zeal and respectability (Gal 1:14). He too needed a "special" conversion, not, perhaps, from moral failures, but from Pharisaism; he needed to be converted from the God of the law to the God of mercy—to

Christ. In the same way, the grumbling Pharisees needed to enter a relationship with Jesus; they needed to turn to him and remain in his presence like the tax collectors and sinners.

As we have already said, this kind of conversion has a second, inseparable dimension, and that is conversion into the community "around Christ." The elder son does not want to go in—to the father, to the younger brother, and to those who are celebrating together—because he harbors resentment toward his brother, and perhaps even more toward his father. Likewise, the Pharisees stay outside the banquet, outside "the church around Christ." But conversion to Christ goes hand in hand with conversion to the community surrounding him, the church. This is not surprising; later, seen through the eyes of the apostle Paul, the church is described as the Body of Christ (see 1 Cor 12:12-27).

The banquet in our parable has clear echoes in the Last Supper, where Jesus says to the apostles, "Take, eat" (Matt 26:26). Here also the father gives, but it is only the younger son who is able to "take and eat." At the beginning he ate without the father, but now, at the banquet, he eats with him; in the far country he had used the father's gifts selfishly and without sharing, but now he is sharing, as part of the community, anticipating the imagery of the Eucharist. The elder brother's problem lies in his inability to take or receive. He lives with his father, whose riches belong to him also, yet he feels like a pauper and so resents his brother. Such a pity, when he too was invited to the banquet!

"Good Christians" and "Bitterness Syndrome"

"Bitterness syndrome" is an unusual syndrome that tends to affect the more zealous, engaged, diligent, and "upright" Christians, in other words those who in many ways resemble the elder son. (If this isn't you, please skip this part!)

Symptoms of Bitterness Syndrome

In the best medical tradition we can create a list of symptoms for this malignant spiritual disease that afflicted the elder son:

- Envy
- Contempt
- Pride
- Anger
- Bitterness
- Jealousy
- Being withdrawn
- Calculation
- Cupidity
- Self-justification
- Self-pity
- Lack of empathy
- Blindness
- Pharisaism

It is hard to believe that this litany of symptoms can be found in the very person who had stayed with the father and enjoyed such a high standard of living. (We can tell from the extravagance of the banquet and the presence of so many servants that the father was far from poor.) But the elder son intrigues us because, yes, seen from the outside, he has always been with the father and has never broken any of his rules; in reality, however, he has never truly been "with" him; otherwise he would not upbraid his father for never having given him so much as a kid that he might "celebrate with [his] friends." Yet the father reassures him that everything—much more than some kid or a fattened calf—was at his disposal. How had he never noticed? Had they not lived together all their lives? But perhaps they lived beside each other yet never truly together, like a husband and wife who live together but do not truly know each other, each leading one's own life, living *beside* each other, but not *together*.

The Inability to Receive

We should ask ourselves how the elder son failed to realize how rich he really was. How could he plead poverty when everything the father owned was his? How could he neither recognize nor receive his father's gifts? The fundamental cause, from which all of the visible symptoms arise, is *egocentrism*, a preoccupation with oneself and one's own accomplishments: "For all these years I have been working like a slave for you . . ." (15:29). The elder son's self-centeredness, for so long submerged, has finally bubbled up to the surface: "yet you have never given me even a young goat." He had been serving the father for his own sake, secretly wishing, waiting, to get something out of him. And here lies the mystery: he had so much more than a simple goat—he had everything—so how could he not realize this? Why did he continue to live like a pauper? The reason is self-centeredness, wanting to *earn* everything and finding it so hard to *receive*.

That the elder son is so closed off and unable to receive is made abundantly clear by his refusal to accept the younger son as his brother: "this son of yours," he says, contemptuously, as if he were nothing to do with him. Locked into his own needs and desires and a sense of righteous anger, he further demonstrates his closed-off nature by staying outside and refusing to go in, showing us that, paradoxically, he too is lost!

We could, therefore, like Bible scholar Paul de Vries, call Luke's story the parable of the Father Who Is Not Lost: the father is the only character who is always there, the only certainty, and an ever-present and overflowing spring of mercy. The only truly "unwavering certainty" is the father's heart, the heart that knows no boundaries, the heart of "limitless mercy."[36] But the only ones who draw from this heart are those who open themselves to it, who *go to it*, not those who stubbornly stay outside.

It is often said that the problem for us Christians is that we cannot give. But the opposite and more relevant problem is equally true: we are unable to receive. It is not surprising therefore that we lack the joy of God's presence. Is this because we are blind and unable to see God's gifts? Is it perhaps because of pride, or the false conviction that in order to receive anything from God we have to *deserve* or *earn* it? Is it because we are not open to, or hungry for, God's gifts? Or is it because of a false sense of self-sufficiency that claims we already have everything we want and everything we need?

If we come to God as people who are rich, who cope with everything and lack nothing, then God and his mercy simply become a kind of "accessory," an optional extra. In which case, why did Christ have to come? And are we like this? Do we lack real hunger for God, the hunger that ate at the younger son?

If so, how can we instill such hunger in ourselves? We need to pray for a genuine desire for God, for his Gift, to hunger and thirst for his presence.

Because he feels that an injustice has been done to him, the elder son maligns his brother and accuses him of having "devoured [his father's] property with prostitutes" (v. 30). But this fact is not mentioned in the earlier narrative so is very likely his own projection, or perhaps a case of *the wish being the father to the thought.* The apostle Paul says that "Love . . . rejoices in the truth" (1 Cor 13:6), but self-love rejoices in the wrong, and derives satisfaction from other people's failures. As Benedict XVI points out, "Their bitterness towards God's goodness reveals an inward bitterness regarding their own obedience, the bitterness that indicates the limitations of this obedience. In their heart of hearts, they would have gladly journeyed out into that great 'freedom' as well. There is an unspoken envy of what others have been able to get away with."[37]

Despite all his faults and failings, the elder son does at least manage to do one good thing (apart from his faithfulness and hard work): he does not keep his bitterness to himself but pours it out, openly, in front of the father. This is very wise, as was shown long ago, in the Old Testament, where the psalmists would "pour out [their] heart" before God (Ps 62:8), handing over to him all their feelings and emotions, even the negative ones such as despair, emptiness, vengefulness, disappointment, and anger.[38] Even though this is not, by itself, sufficient medicine for a complete cure, it does at least provide some kind of "analgesic." It is important to note, however, that the psalmists rarely stop at their lament, but add words of hope and have faith that God will intervene and change their fate.

The psalmists' faith is so strong that even in the midst of difficulties and unresolved problems they are certain that change will come. The prime example of this is probably the best known of all the psalms of lament, the psalm that the evangelist puts into the mouth of the crucified Christ, Psalm 22. A lengthy litany of sorrows is followed by an astonishing turnaround when the psalmist expresses his conviction that he will yet glorify God's name:

> I will tell of your name to my brothers and sisters;
>> in the midst of the congregation I will praise you:
> You who fear the LORD, praise him!
>> All you offspring of Jacob, glorify him;
>> stand in awe of him, all you offspring of Israel!
> For he did not despise or abhor the affliction of the
>> afflicted;
> he did not hide his face from me,
>> but heard when I cried to him.
> From you comes my praise in the great congregation;
>> my vows I will pay before those who fear him.
> The poor shall eat and be satisfied;
>> those who seek him shall praise the LORD.
> May your hearts live forever! (Ps 22:22-26)

This is the vision of someone genuinely full of faith, who with the freedom of a child of God pours out his heart before him, but who is also certain in his hope that God will take care of him! This firm hope is what the psalmists express in their hymns of praise, which burst forth *in anticipation* of God's intervention.

The Elder Son in Us

We do not need to look for the elder son only in the virtual world of the biblical story—we can find him in ourselves too. In us he lives, speaks, grumbles, but wants to stay excluded, alone in his defiance and disappointment. There can be a variety of reasons for this: Why didn't God take care of me in this situation? Why are the people around me doing so well even though spiritually they're not trying as hard as I am? Why isn't God blessing me as much as those who have only just been converted? Why do the people around me experience prayer as a joyful meeting with the Lord and feel his love and presence, while I, even though I have been trying faithfully for many years, am experiencing only a wilderness? Prayer—and the Christian life in general—remain for me a bare and joyless duty. And my service . . . I've been toiling away for years in the parish community but I'm not getting as much recognition as others who have been doing so much less than I have. And why do "the youth," or at least those younger than me, who have less experience by far than I have, always seem to get priority treatment? Why don't they respect me and ask for my advice? I've been trying my best for years, and all I get is hard work and drudgery, not a scrap of sympathy, and not so much as a "goat."

Inspired by the elder son, Henri Nouwen offers a telling insight into such introspection:

> When I listen carefully to the words with which the elder son attacks his father—self-righteous, self-pitying, jealous words—I hear a deeper complaint. It is the complaint that comes from a heart that feels it never received what it was due. . . . It is the complaint that cries out: "I tried so hard, worked so long, did so much, and still I have not received what others get so easily. Why do people not thank me, not invite me, not play with me, not honor me, while they pay so much attention to those who take life so easily and so casually?"

It is in this spoken or unspoken complaint that I recognize the elder son in me. Often I catch myself complaining about little rejections, little impolitenesses, little negligences. Time and again I discover within me that murmuring, whining, grumbling, lamenting, and griping that go on and on even against my will. The more I dwell on the matters in question, the worse my state becomes. The more I analyze it, the more reason I see for complaint. And the more deeply I enter it, the more complicated it gets. There is an enormous, dark drawing power to this inner complaint. Condemnation of others, and self-condemnation, self-righteousness and self-rejection keep reinforcing each other in an ever more vicious way. Every time I allow myself to be seduced by it, it spins me down in an endless spiral of self-rejection. As I let myself be drawn into the vast interior labyrinth of my complaints, I become more and more lost until, in the end, I feel myself to be the most misunderstood, rejected, neglected, and despised person in the world.

Of one thing I am sure. Complaining is self-perpetuating and counterproductive. . . . A complainer is hard to live with, and very few people know how to respond to the complaints made by a self-rejecting person.[39]

How to "Cure" the Elder Son

Now that we have established our diagnosis, it should be a simple matter to find the appropriate treatment. We can start with the father's words, "all that is mine is yours" (v. 31). It is interesting that the father does not tell his protesting elder son to try harder, to stop whining, and to stop being so envious and self-pitying, but instead opens his son's eyes to see how blessed he really is. He very calmly, with no sign of offense or agitation, says, "all that is mine is yours." And *all* does not mean *only some things*! We hear the same words in Jesus' "farewell" prayer in which he expresses his relationship with his Father and his disciples: "All mine are yours, and yours are mine" (John 17:10). In his conversation with the younger son, the father does not respond directly or give a thought-out reply: he simply *gives*. It is the same in his conversation with the elder son when he goes out to plead with him: he reassures him that he too has "plenty," and invites him to come in and celebrate.

A workable prototype of the elder son can be found in the life of the prophet Jonah, who is no common "godless sinner," but is a religious Jew (Jonah 1:9) who has no wish to accept a new direction from God. Furthermore, like the Pharisees who were amazed at Jesus' behavior, he does not wish to learn God's compassion, or, like the elder son, share it with others. So he runs away, just like Adam (see Gen 3:8-10), from God and from his Word (Jonah 1:3), which makes it all the more surprising that he still considers himself to be a man who fears the Lord! Jonah's flight finishes with his discovery that it is impossible to run away from God and hide (Jonah 2:1-11; Ps 139:1-12); such attempts are a "vanity of vanities" (Eccl 1:2).

Neither can the elder son "escape" from the father. But notice how the father's behavior toward the elder son differs from his behavior toward the younger, "prodigal" son. He does not embrace the elder son; he does not kiss him. Why is this? Perhaps because he knew he would meet with the same reaction we encounter when we are kind to an angry person: kindness causes even more anger. The younger son *was already open to accept the father* (and to allow himself to be accepted by him);

the elder son is not yet ready to do this. What this shows us is the appropriateness of God's call and self-giving: he gives himself according to a person's ability to hear him and accept him, as in the parable of the Talents, where he gave "to each according to his ability" (Matt 25:15).

Whenever the "elder son" (hidden in us) takes hold of us, we can use, as the perfect remedy, the father's words, "all that is mine is yours"! Jesus is here, all for us! The Trinity is here, all for us! There is no greater gift! And with this Gift come every manner of smaller gifts, "bonuses," which Paul describes in his letter to the Ephesians, and whenever we feel we are "just poor Christians," we can find this passage and dwell on the words of such a magnificent hymn of praise:

> Blessed be the God and Father of our Lord Jesus Christ, who has blessed us in Christ with every spiritual blessing in the heavenly places, just as he chose us in Christ before the foundation of the world to be holy and blameless before him in love. He destined us for adoption as his children through Jesus Christ, according to the good pleasure of his will, to the praise of his glorious grace that he freely bestowed on us in the Beloved. In him we have redemption through his blood, the forgiveness of our trespasses, according to the riches of his grace that he lavished on us. With all wisdom and insight he has made known to us the mystery of his will, according to his good pleasure that he set forth in Christ, as a plan for the fullness of time, to gather up all things in him, things in heaven and things on earth. In Christ we have also obtained an inheritance, having been destined according to the purpose of him who accomplishes all things according to his counsel and

> will, so that we, who were the first to set our hope on Christ, might live for the praise of his glory. In him you also, when you had heard the word of truth, the gospel of your salvation, and had believed in him, were marked with the seal of the promised Holy Spirit; this is the pledge of our inheritance toward redemption as God's own people, to the praise of his glory. (Eph 1:3-14)

So giving thanks, we burst forth with joy: we are richer than we thought! We do not have to survive on the pods the pigs are eating—God is setting before us a table laid out for a feast. And we know we can truly be healed of our discontent because giving thanks is itself an effective cure for our bitterness. Of course, it is easy to agree with these fine words when we read them in a book; it is more difficult in the grim reality of everyday life. Nonetheless, even then, "Though the fig tree does not blossom, / and no fruit is on the vines" (Hab 3:17), we can still proclaim our trust in God's faithfulness. During the Mass we hear, "It is truly right and just . . . always and everywhere to give you thanks." Even when we feel not a single drop of consolation from God, at all times and in all places we can give thanks because God is faithful, and his "yes" toward us *remains*; it is unchanging, just as the apostle Paul affirms: "For the Son of God, Jesus Christ, whom we proclaimed among you, Silvanus and Timothy and I, was not 'Yes and No'; but in him it is always 'Yes'" (2 Cor 1:19).

There is another practical way to receive the riches we have in the Lord, and that is to allow ourselves, after receiving the sacrament of reconciliation or the Eucharist, or during prayer, to simply enjoy the fact that the Father has blessed us, that he has given us himself, to enjoy it, plainly and simply, just as we enjoy a delicious meal. Rest, wonder . . . and after a while deep gratitude and inner praise may arise. If our life with Christ is based only on achievements, even in prayer, then it is no wonder that after a while we become afflicted by elder son syndrome and give in to discontent and frustration. From time to time we need to celebrate, to rest, to "allow ourselves to be loved more," as Elizabeth of the Trinity might have urged us, to experience that "all that belongs to Jesus belongs to us," even that "all of Jesus" is for us.

Differences between the Two Brothers

The motif of "two brothers" appears a number of times in the Bible: from Cain and Abel, Ishmael and Isaac, and Esau and Jacob in the Old Testament, to the parables of the New Testament (see Matt 21:28-32). The two brothers in our story display several contrasting characteristics:

The younger son	The elder son
Wastes everything	Everything the father has is his also
Leaves for a "distant country"	Stays with the father
Breaks the relationship of respect	Never breaks anything
Arises and goes to his father	Stays outside
Confesses his sin	Self-confidently professes his "sinlessness"
Humble, open	Angry, envious, closed off and withdrawn
Uses the name "father"—personal	Avoids the name "father" and talks about his brother as "this son of yours"—impersonal

The elder son's antisocial attitude is shown by his excluding himself, his staying outside. He does not "know" the father. He does not, unlike the younger son, even call him "father," nor does he use the word "brother," simply alluding to "This son of yours." Our story has echoes in the parable of the Pharisee and the Tax Collector (see Luke 18:10-14). Just as the elder son speaks of "this son of yours" and never having "disobeyed your command," the Pharisee declares, "I am not like other people: thieves, rogues, adulterers, or even like this tax collector" (18:11). The younger son, meanwhile, even though his own motives are ambiguous, reminds us of the tax collector, who cries, "God, be merciful to me, a sinner!" (18:13). The father still considers the elder son to be his son, however, even though the corresponding relationship is missing. He even calls him "my child,"[40] an even more affectionate and emotionally stronger address than "son." He also reminds this "child" of his that "the other" is still his brother.[41]

Similarities between the Two Brothers

As well as contrasting characteristics, the two brothers in our parable have several features in common:

1. They have a false and distorted image of the father.
   Neither of them has an image of the father as good: the younger son runs away from him; the elder son reproaches him, wrongly, for not being generous enough to him.

2. They run away from the father.
   They do not want to have anything to do with him: the younger son runs away; the elder son stays outside and avoids using the word "father."

3. They experience a crisis while they are "away" from the father.
   The younger son experiences hunger and humiliation; the elder son stays outside, angry, grumbling, and inwardly unhappy.

4. They look after their own interests.
   They do not care about the father: the younger son asks for his share of the inheritance; the elder son reproaches his father for never having given him anything.

5. They lack a genuine father-son relationship.
   The younger son leaves the father, and his return is motivated by self-love; the elder son is more like a hired workman, more concerned about reward than a relationship.

Both sons need to leave behind the attitude of a "servant-opportunist" and rediscover their "sonship"; they both need to be converted, from the mentality of a hired workman to that of a true son. (It is true that the younger son took a step toward conversion, but it was only the first of many.) Through his presence and his word the father leads his younger and elder sons toward conversion, and it is important to notice that it is the *father* who reveals *to them* the possibility—the necessity—of a change of heart. Without the father's word, the younger son would have remained one of the servants, as he had requested; likewise, the elder son would have remained "outside."

Here we are touching on a fundamental truth: that conversion is a gift from God! Without God, we do not even know from what, and to what, we need to turn, and our outlook remains "human, all too human,"[42] or not even that. It is God's presence, God's word, that leads to the real Copernican shift.

It has now become abundantly clear that the familiar title for the parable—the Prodigal Son—is far from the most fitting: the main character is the father, not the younger son; the lives of the younger and elder sons depend completely on the father, who always has the final say; it is the father who is prodigal, giving freely and generously to both sons; and both sons are, in contrast to the father, selfish and calculating. Perhaps, then, the most appropriate title would be something like, "the parable of the Prodigal Father and the Ungrateful (Selfish) Sons."[43]

The Parable of Liberation

Liberation theology has recently become (at least in some circles) quite a fashionable topic for debate. We can certainly find the theology of liberation in our parable—liberation from attitudes unworthy of human beings, and which have no place in the life of a Christian disciple.

It is a parable of liberation from:

- Misery and poverty, both internal (emptiness and anger) and external.

- A "state of estrangement": neither the younger nor the elder son see themselves as part of a family.

- A burdensome past.

- Hardness of heart (in the case of the elder son): twice we hear the refrain (at the end of the respective passage), "this son of mine [brother of yours] was dead and is alive again; he was lost and is found!" (15:24; see 15:32). The father intends this statement to soften the heart of, and evoke a sense of solidarity in, the elder brother.

- Sadness, and being closed off to the joy of sharing (with the father and with others).
- The "mask" of the good and model Christian.
- Egocentrism. Liberation comes through allowing oneself to be "infected" with the example of the father, who is the very opposite of egocentric.

Essentially, all of these points relate to *liberation from self-centeredness* in all its many forms. We find the same issues addressed in Paul's letters, especially Romans 6–8 and Galatians 5, where we are emphatically reminded that true Christian freedom is freedom *from* egocentrism *to* Christocentrism; from a life focused on ourselves and our sinful desires to a life focused on Christ and his way. So, going back to our parable, if the father represents Christ, then both sons are invited to accept liberation from living life for themselves to living life with Christ.

Living for God . . . for One's Own Sake?

The elder son is a prime example of how it is possible to live for the father—for God—for one's own sake, and this practice is not as rare as we might think. How often do we seek out God only because we have an intractable problem, or because we simply need help? At such times we are seeking him only in order to get something out of him: for us the Lord becomes the doctor, the odd-job man, our servant. It can be the same in our service for Christ: we can be serving him because it brings us pleasure, because we find having power over others intoxicating, or because we are attracted by a sense of our own importance and fascinated by our own achievements and abilities. And all of this is amplified when people shower us with words of appreciation. Oswald Chambers rightly said that "the greatest competitor of devotion to Jesus is service for Him."[44] Prayer, Christian service, listening to sermons, and dwelling on God's word can all become "instruments" in this way, simply devices for filling up an empty emotional reservoir or for satisfying our curiosity.

Of course, we all need to experience tangible blessings from God and from other people—gratitude, support, and appreciation. But questions remain: What is most important for us? Are we able to serve God and live for him even without these "goats"? Or does the thought of service without reward evoke feelings of bitterness and discontentment? Although it was the spiritual giant and missionary Francis Xavier who confidently asserted, "Were there no heaven to gain, nor hell to flee, I would still love thee,"[45] this is something into which we mere mortals do need to grow. Are we able to serve even though we are not currently receiving a "goat," or a fatted calf, or a new robe, or a ring? Are we able to live a life of devotion to God even when we are not experiencing any enjoyment from prayer or from service to others, and feel we are not achieving anything or receiving any appreciation? And, finally, how can we tell whether our service is truly altruistic (that is, performed for God and others) or comes with ulterior motives that may be deeply hidden? We will know the answer as soon as we hear music from a celebration that is in full flow, but which is being thrown for somebody else. Do we feel sad and envious because it is not for us? Or are we happy that there is a celebration for our brother or sister?

Common Riches

It is said that if, in a marriage, we start to weigh up which partner is giving more, this could mean the beginning of the end. Making such comparisons is, however, the elder son's greatest fault. It is always misleading to compare ourselves with others, to count how much we are getting and how much they are getting, from God or from other people. The life of the prophet Jonah once more anticipates the attitude of the elder son in that when the Ninevites change their ways and gain a reprieve from God, Jonah, instead of being happy at the fortune of others, is upset and angry (see Jonah 4:1-3). Unbelievable! But no—perhaps in light of our own experience we can understand this, at least a little. Are we able to be sincerely joyful over the gifts our brothers and sisters receive from the Lord? Are we? Even when we stay "unnoticed" by people and seemingly by God as well? We should not be looking for God's riches in our lives only, but also in the lives of our Christian brothers and sisters! We can and should take joy from what God gives to others as if they were our own gifts! This is exactly what the father urges his elder son to do when he invites him in to the banquet: to rejoice with those who rejoice (see Rom 12:15). Aelred of Rievaulx offers some beautiful words on the subject of taking joy from the blessings others receive:

> No one therefore should boast on his own about any grace given by God as if it were exclusively his own. No one should envy his brother because of some grace, as if it were exclusively his. Whatever he has, he should appreciate it and consider it for the good of all his brothers, and whatever his brother has, he should never doubt is also

his. God in his caring way of dealing with us causes each
person to need the other and to have in the other what one
does not possess in oneself. Thus humility is preserved,
charity increased and unity recognized! Let the weak say:
I am strong! When the strong brother beside him suffers
of his weakness, he is made strong by the strength of his
brother![46]

Elder brother syndrome shows itself most clearly when we fail to
receive any thanks, or simply when we fail. These words provide
a source of encouragement for such moments:

People are unreasonable, illogical, and self-centered,
LOVE THEM ANYWAY
If you do good, people will accuse you of
selfish, ulterior motives,
DO GOOD ANYWAY
If you are successful,
you win false friends and true enemies,
SUCCEED ANYWAY
The good you do will be forgotten tomorrow,
DO GOOD ANYWAY
Honesty and frankness make you vulnerable,
BE HONEST AND FRANK ANYWAY
What you spent years building may be
destroyed overnight,
BUILD ANYWAY

People really need help
but may attack you if you help them,
HELP PEOPLE ANYWAY
Give the world the best you have
And you'll get kicked in the teeth,
GIVE THE WORLD THE BEST YOU'VE GOT ANYWAY.[47]

If serving in such a selfless way is still too difficult for us, just knowing that with Jesus none of our "hidden" service or endeavors will ever be forgotten will be support enough for us. "The good you do today, will often be forgotten. Do good anyway."

Obstacles to Accepting the "Younger Brother"

When we read the parable of the two brothers, we subconsciously cheer for the elder and somehow fail to understand the younger. In the church, however, we see a lack of acceptance of whole swathes of people, not just model "sinners" but all those Christians with different beliefs and practices from ours. There are at least three obstacles to accepting the "younger brother."

Different Practice

I may know some brothers who are "weak in faith" and whose way of life in Christ I do not fully share. But who knows how God sees them? Perhaps it is me who is the weaker! In his letter to the Romans, the apostle Paul gives some practical advice on dealing with such relationships:

Welcome those who are weak in faith, but not for the purpose of quarreling over opinions. (Rom 14:1)

So then, each of us will be accountable to God. Let us therefore no longer pass judgment on one another, but resolve instead never to put a stumbling block or hindrance in the way of another. (Rom 14:12-13)

Let us then pursue what makes for peace and for mutual upbuilding. (Rom 14:19)

We who are strong ought to put up with the failings of the weak, and not to please ourselves. Each of us must please our neighbor for the good purpose of building up the neighbor. For Christ did not please himself. (Rom 15:1-3a)

"Higher Knowledge"

In the early days of Christianity, Johannine communities in the area surrounding Ephesus in what is now Southwestern Turkey experienced a number of divisions and schisms. A group of Christians split off from them because they believed they had "higher knowledge," lived a fuller Christian life, and enjoyed a more perfect union with God.[48] The author of the First Letter of John responded to this problem, seeing the roots of the division in, among other things, the lack of concrete love that the seemingly "advanced Christians" showed toward the "little children" to whom the letter is addressed. This is in fact only a variation on the familiar conflict in the gospels between the "perfect Pharisees" and "weaker tax collectors." Deeper knowledge of God cannot in reality, however, separate us from the "less perfect" (see 1 John 4:7-12, 19-21).

Sinfulness

In the words of Saint Augustine, we need to "love the sinner and hate the sin" (see also Rev 2:2-6).[49] This is, admittedly, quite difficult, and we often slip into one or other of the extremes: either we advocate so-called Irenicism—artificial peace and limitless tolerance—or we veer toward intolerance and a Pharisaic separation from the "imperfect." The ideal, however, is to "speak the truth in love" (see Eph 4:15).

Deciding for . . . the Prodigal Father

Our parable is open-ended. We do not know if the elder son accepted the father's invitation: the answer is deliberately withheld so that those who hear (or read) the story must decide for themselves. Because eating together was a sign of community, accepting the father's invitation means accepting the younger brother as well as the father, and complete acceptance of the father means accepting his lifestyle and his attitudes.

So the greatest challenge is saved until last. Pauline Marie Jaricot, the founder of the Society for the Propagation of the Faith, wrote, "If only I could love without measure . . . without end."[50] In the same spirit, Saint Bernard suggests that since "God is both infinite and immeasurable," any love offered to God should likewise be "infinite and immeasurable."[51] How can we achieve this? Well, perhaps if we grow to truly admire the prodigal father, we will become like him—after all, "love assimilates"—and in so doing we will come to love Jesus himself, who is symbolized by the father.

We can also try to understand how the prodigal Father behaves toward us personally, to meditate on his compassion, to watch him, again and again, come out to meet us and give us a new robe and a ring—give us everything he has. But simply "pondering" this goodness of his is insufficient. We need to accept it, especially into those places where we are less able to open ourselves up to his mercy, into those areas where the "bad father" resides, the one who never indulges us, who keeps a tight rein on us, who gives us "a snake" when we ask for "a fish" (Luke 11:11), who tyrannizes by his "merciless demands," and who is interested only in our achievements, wanting more and more yet never being satisfied.

Do we sometimes live before the "terrible face" of this merciless God? The parable urges us to turn around and leave this image behind, to allow God to change it. Jesus reveals God, *who is compassionate, who gives in abundance.* The degree to which we accept his compassion (not abstractly or intellectually, but concretely) is the degree to which we can give it away. But to accept his compassion does not mean only to accept his gifts but, first and foremost, to allow ourselves to be transformed by his "compassionate heart," to become as compassionate as he is. We have already said that God's compassion begins "inside," in the depths of God's being, and this is exactly where compassion needs to begin in us as well.

This is why, in his letter to the Colossians, Paul says, "*accept* a compassionate heart" (Col 3:12; NRSV: "*clothe* yourselves . . ."). Paul is not urging us to *perform* acts of compassion but to *accept* a "compassionate heart," from which all the concrete attitudes will spring: kindness, tolerance, forgiveness, forbearance. True acceptance of this compassion, into our whole heart, will automatically show itself on the outside and this will be proof of real "inwardness." In the words of Meister Eckhart's spiritual heir, Henry Suso: "Whoever has inwardness in outward affairs, his inwardness will become more inward than someone's whose inwardness is only in inward matters."[52]

To accept God's "compassionate heart," to allow God's Spirit to transform us from the inside—this appeal is addressed to us as well. Before God's face we can put away our "uncompassionate heart" and accept God's fatherly (and motherly) heart. We need to welcome the "transplanting" of this heart: it is an operation we need to undergo again and again, and which will save our life and the lives of those we love. The new heart will enable us to live like the prodigal father, who in his compassion without measure also displays so many motherly characteristics. We will then be able to pour out our heart of compassion, for the young and the old, the weak and the strong, the broken and the bitter, just like the generous father in the parable. Just like Jesus.

Blessed be those who accept—and continue to accept—God's mercy, for they will be merciful!

Notes

Introduction

1. "Scriba mansuetudinis Christi"; see Dante Alighieri, *De Monarchia*, 1:16. One English translation reads: "The writer of the gentleness of Christ"; see *The De Monarchia of Dante Alighieri,* trans. Aurelia Henry (Boston: Houghton, Mifflin, 1904), 61.

2. Josef Schmid, *Das Evangelium nach Lukas*, RNT 3 (Regensburg: F. Pustet, 1955), 252; Adolf Jülicher, *Die Gleichnisreden Jesu II: Auslegung der Gleichnisreden der drei ersten Evangelien* (Darmstadt: Wissenschaftliche Buchgesellschaft, 1963), 334.

3. Graham Greene, *Monsignor Quixote* (London: Vintage, 2000), 59–62.

1 The Context of the Story

1. See Joachim Jeremias, *The Parables of Jesus,* 3rd ed. (London: SCM, 1972), 131–32.

2. St. Therese of Lisieux, Doctor of the Church, understood this parable in the same way. See Therese of Lisieux, *Autobiography of a Saint* (London: Harvill, 1958), 312. This interpretation is also advocated by Benedict XVI; see *Jesus of Nazareth* (London: Bloomsbury, 2007), 207–8, citing the French biblical scholar Grelot.

2 The Structure of the Parable

1. This is exactly in the spirit of Luke's frequent use of *synkrisis* (parallelism, juxtaposition of characters and concepts). See Jean-Noel Aletti, *Il Racconto Come Teologia* (Roma: Edizioni Dehoniane, 1996), 56–57.

2. See Michel Gourgues, *Le Parabole di Luca* (Torino: Elledici, 1998), 123–25.

3. If a parable has two climaxes, the emphasis is usually on the second; see Jeremias, *The Parables of Jesus*, 131.

3 Interpretation and Application of the Parable

1. See Joseph Fitzmyer, *The Gospel According to Luke X–XXIV* (Garden City, NY: Doubleday, 1985), 1087.

2. Raniero Cantalamessa, *Life in the Lordship of Christ* (Kansas City, MO: Sheed and Ward, 1990). The root of all sin is ungodliness (Greek, *asebeia*), living without God, as if God did not exist.

3. See Michel Gourgues, *Le Parabole di Luca* (Torino: Elledici, 1998), 131.

4. It is only the elder son who says the younger son "devoured [the father's] property with prostitutes." See Luke 15:30.

5. Timothy Keller, *The Prodigal God* (New York: Dutton, 2008), 46.

6. See André Louf, *Sotto la Guida dello Spirito* (Bose: Qiqajon Edizioni, 1990), 23.

7. Ibid.

8. Benedict XVI, *Jesus of Nazareth*, 204.

9. "Can't Get Away," words by Mark Heimermann, appears on John Schlitt, *Unfit for Swine* (Word Records, 1996).

10. Benedict XVI, *Jesus of Nazareth*, 204–5.

11. Saint Augustine, *Confessions* 10.27.

12. Benedict XVI, *Jesus of Nazareth*, 205.

13. Another possible reaction to the "spinning wheels" is resignation, or passively accepting the status quo without expecting any change in the situation.

14. The Greek text talks about a literal "piercing" of the heart, while ecumenical translations talk more subtly about "striking."

15. St. Isaac of Syria, *The Ascetical Homilies of Saint Isaac the Syrian* 64 (Boston: Holy Transfiguration Monastery, 1984), 317. See also Hilarion Alfeyev, *The Spiritual World of Isaac the Syrian*, Cistercian Studies 175 (Collegeville, MN: Cistercian Publications, 2000), 132.

16. The Hebrew text allows for several possible translations. A similar translation to that here is in the German liturgical Bible, the *Einheitsübersetzung*, which has: "Führ mich zurück, umkehren will ich."

17. Or untamable, not able to be trained for the yolk, left at the mercy of its own whims, passions, and moods (anger, fretfulness, aloofness).

18. Henri Nouwen, *The Return of the Prodigal Son* (New York: Doubleday, 1994), 106.

19. See "Letter to Roland, 23 June 1896," *Collected Letters of Saint Therese of Lisieux* (London: Sheed and Ward, 1949), 236.

20. Anthropomorphism is the attribution of human characteristics and behavior to God himself. Literally, personification.

21. St. Isaac of Syria, *The Ascetical Homilies of Saint Isaac the Syrian*, 244.

22. Archimandrite Sophrony, *Wisdom from Mount Athos: The Writings of Staretz Silouan* (Crestwood, NY: St. Vladimir's Seminary Press, 2001).

23. The father does not respond directly to his son's confession ("I am no longer worthy to be called your son") but, indirectly, affirms that he had never stopped being his son ("for this *son* of mine was dead").

24. St. Therese of Lisieux, *Autobiography of a Saint* (London: Harvill, 1958), 312.

25. St. Bernard of Clairvaux, Sermon 83, *On the Song of Songs*, vol. 4 (Kalamazoo, MI: Cistercian Publications, 1980), 184.

26. Elizabeth of the Trinity, *The Praise of Glory: Reminiscences of Sister Elizabeth of the Trinity*, trans. Benedictines of Stanbrook (Westminster, MD: Newman, 1962).

27. Ibid.

28. See Søren Kierkegaard, *Upbuilding Discourses in Various Spirits* (Princeton: Princeton University Press, 2009).

29. Elizabeth of the Trinity, *The Praise of Glory*, 251.

30. Ibid., 266.

31. See Hans Urs von Balthasar, *Love Alone Is Credible*, trans. D. C. Schindler (San Francisco: Ignatius, 2004); see also Balthasar, *Theodrama: Theological Dramatic Theory*, vol. 4: *The Action* (San Francisco: Ignatius, 1994), 325–27.

32. See Dietrich Bonhoeffer, *The Cost of Discipleship* (London: SCM Press, 1959), 35–37. The introductory words in this chapter are very strong: "Cheap grace is the deadly enemy of our Church. We are fighting today for costly grace" (35).

33. The Greek word *apollymi* can mean both "to become (or be) lost" or "to perish."

34. See Benedict XVI, *Jesus of Nazareth*, 209.

35. Ibid., 210–11.

36. See Nouwen, *The Return of the Prodigal Son*, 75.

37. Benedict XVI, *Jesus of Nazareth*, 211.

38. In connection with this it is impossible not to recall "blameless and upright" Job, who finds himself in a similar situation to the elder son, standing face-to-face with God's incomprehensible ways, which differed so much from what he expected. His reaction is also similar: anger, bitterness, reproach.

39. Nouwen, *The Return of the Prodigal Son*, 72–73.

40. He does not say "son" (Luke 15:31; ecumenical translation), which is a weak and inaccurate translation of the Greek word *teknon*.

41. See Gourgues, *Le Parabole di Luca*, 136.

42. In this phrase, Nietzsche, in his book of the same title, criticizes the superficial nature of the "Christian" lives of his contemporaries.

43. See Gourgues, *Le Parabole di Luca*, 126–27.

44. Cited in Leanne Payne, *Listening Prayer* (Grand Rapids, MI: Baker, 1994).

45. From a translation of the sixteenth-century hymn "O Deus, ego amo te."

46. Aelred of Rievaulx, Sermon 7, cited by Daniel Ange, *Kdo je Můj Bratr?* (Kostelní Vydří: Karmelitánské nakladatelství, 2010), 173.

47. Adapted from Kent M. Keith, "The Paradoxical Commandments." Reported in *Mother Teresa: A Simple Path*, compiled by Lucinda Vardey (New York: Ballantine Books, 1995), 185. Vardey said that it was "a sign on the wall of Shishu Bhavan, the children's home in Calcutta."

48. See Raymond Brown, *An Introduction to the New Testament* (New York: Doubleday, 1997), 389–92.

49. See Saint Augustine, Letter 211 in *Letters*, vol. 5, *204–270*, trans. Wilfrid Parsons, The Fathers of the Church 32 (Washington, DC: The Catholic University of America Press, 1956), 46.

50. See Society for the Propagation of the Faith, One Family in Mission, http://www.onefamilyinmission.org/society-propfaith/paulinejaricot.html.

51. Bernard of Clairvaux, *On Loving God* 6.16.

52. Quoted in *Henry Suso: The Exemplar, with Two German Sermons*, trans. and ed. Frank Tobin, Classics of Western Spirituality (New York: Paulist, 1989), 184.

Bibliography

Aletti, Jean-Noel. *Il Racconto Come Teologia*. Roma: Edizioni Dehoniane, 1996.

Alfeyev, Hilarion. *The Spiritual World of Isaac the Syrian*. Cistercian
Studies 175. Collegeville, MN: Cistercian Publications, 2000.

Ange, Daniel. *Kdo je Můj Bratr?* Kostelní Vydří: Karmelitánské nakladatelství, 2010.

Augustine. *Confessions*. Translated by Henry Chadwick. Oxford: Oxford University Press, 2008.

———. *Letters*. Vol. 5, *204-270*. Translated by Wilfrid Parsons. The
Fathers of the Church 32. Washington, DC: The Catholic University
of America Press, 1956.

Balthasar, Hans Urs von. *Glaubhaft ist nur Liebe*. Einsiedeln: Johannes
Verlag, 1963.

———. *Theodramatik III. Die Handlung*. Einsiedeln: Johannes Verlag,
1980.

Benedict XVI. *Jesus of Nazareth: From the Baptism in the Jordan to
the Transfiguration*. London: Bloomsbury, 2007.

Bernard of Clairvaux. *On Loving God*, Cistercian Fathers Series 13B
Kalamazoo, MI: Cistercian Publications, 1995.

———. *On the Song of Songs*. Vol. 4. Translated by Irene Edmonds.
Cistercian Fathers Series 40. Kalamazoo, MI: Cistercian Publications, 1980.

Bonhoeffer, Dietrich. *The Cost of Discipleship*. London: SCM Press,
1959.

Brown, Raymond. *An Introduction to the New Testament*, New York: Doubleday, 1997.

Cantalamessa, Raniero. *Life in the Lordship of Christ.* Kansas City, MO: Sheed and Ward, 1990.

Elizabeth of the Trinity. *The Praise of Glory: Reminiscences of Sister Elizabeth of the Trinity.* Translated by the Benedictines of Stanbrook. Westminster, MD: Newman, 1962.

Fitzmyer, Joseph. *The Gospel According to Luke (X–XXIV).* Garden City, NY: Doubleday, 1985.

Gourgues, Michel. *Le Parabole di Luca.* Torino: Elledici, 1998.

Greene, Graham. *Monsignor Quixote.* London: Vintage, 2000.

Henry, Aurelia, trans. *The De Monarchia of Dante Alighieri.* Boston: Houghton, Mifflin, 1904.

Isaac of Syria, Saint. *The Ascetical Homilies of Saint Isaac the Syrian.* Boston: Holy Transfiguration Monastery, 1984.

Jeremias, Joachim. *The Parables of Jesus.* 3rd ed. London: SCM: 1972.

Jülicher, Adolf. *Die Gleichnisreden Jesu II: Auslegung der Gleichnisreden der drei ersten Evangelien.* Darmstadt: Wissenschaftliche Buchgesellschaft, 1963.

Keller, Timothy. *The Prodigal God.* New York: Dutton, 2008.

Kierkegaard, Søren. *Upbuilding Discourses in Various Spirits.* Princeton: Princeton University Press, 2009.

Louf, André. *Sotto la Guida dello Spirito.* Bose: Qiqajon Edizioni, 1990.

Nouwen, Henri. *The Return of the Prodigal Son.* New York: Doubleday, 1994.

Payne, Leanne. *Listening Prayer.* Grand Rapids, MI: Baker, 1994.

Schmid, Josef. *Das Evangelium nach Lukas.* RNT 3. Regensburg: F. Pustet, 1955.

Society for the Propagation of the Faith. One Family in Mission. http://www.onefamilyinmission.org/society-propfaith/paulinejaricot.html.

Sophrony, Archimandrite. *Wisdom from Mount Athos: The Writings of Staretz Silouan.* Crestwood, NY: St. Vladimir's Seminary Press, 2001.

Suso, Henry. *Henry Suso: The Exemplar, with Two German Sermons.* Translated and edited by Frank Tobin. Classics of Western Spirituality. New York: Paulist, 1989.

Therese of Lisieux. *Autobiography of a Saint.* London: Harvill, 1958.

———. *Collected Letters.* London: Sheed and Ward, 1949.